Praise

MW01145876

Marie DiMenna's book was both calming and inspiring to read. Kindness is the theme, how to be kind to yourself and others in order to create a more beautiful world. Loving ourselves is not easy, but it begins with kindness, caring compassion. Simple poems of giving and receiving kindness point the way toward the world we wish to create. The effect is to reassure us that we can do this, that every thought and every act counts. As Marie writes, 'Breathe in the compassionate world we are co-creating. Breathe out all that does not serve us.' The last section is stunningly beautiful poems from Marie's mystical experiences. Again, they are simple but they go deep. I will use them as prayers as I weave the sacred cloth of my garden and the surrounding forest.

> Caitlin Adair, nature-mystic and author of *Love's Body Speaks*

Truthful, passionate, inspiring and contemplative. *Fierce Compassion, Deep Devotion* lives up to its name.

> Rt. Reverend Cara Cairo, Master and Independent Bishop

In "A Recovery Poem," the opening poem of *Fierce Compassion, Deep Devotion*, "We Recover" is an anthem, a call, to step into a universal truth which perpetually sustains and inspires. In these words, we find acknowledgement and hope. We understand fortitude as embodied love. These poems are like compassionate sermons, in which Marie DiMenna exhorts us to step boldly into new life. Silently, we cry, "Amen" and allow ourselves to be inspired.

Carol Rathe, Christian Mystic and Progressive

This is poetry for these modern times and the very real issues we face today--racial discrimination, political discord, wealth inequality, mental health, democracy, and more. But as refreshingly as the poems address these problems unflinchingly, they also contain an undercurrent of compassion and kindness. As the book continues, the poems turn inward toward the mystic's heart, reveling in the beloved truth of God's love. In poems like "Life is a Bed of Roses," DiMenna takes on a Rumi-like playfulness, "Whoever told you, 'Life isn't a bed of roses,' lied to your face." In others, she takes us into her heart, which is clearly filled with devotion for God, Jesus, and Mother Mary. These poems are meant to be held, contemplated, and explored. Through them, we can find the peace and joy that Christ promises us, and hope that love will indeed conquer the problems that our humanity is grappling with.

Timothy Lin, Founder of Egoless Life Coaching

What a joy to read Marie DiMenna's words and feel her heart and soul in them! Her passion and compassion, devotion and dedication all shine through her words. Marie's love of words is apparent, along with her desire to serve and uplift others in their journeys. She gives us the fruits of her contemplations on life, justice, peace and God's merciful Love...all things we would benefit from contemplating more often.

Fierce Compassion, Deep Devotion is stunning. I love the poems. and theme. I really hope this goes far and wide!

Fierce Compassion, Deep Devotion unites us in the service of healing both ourselves and the great pain in our world through love. "Let go of judgment and be present to the unfolding journey of your soul's knowing" and to join as "a non-violent army of love". Knit together by vulnerability and courage she presses us to see and to share the love of the source that is "changeless and calm".

Reading and exploring Marie DiMenna's book of poetry, *Fierce Compassion, Deep Devotion Poems for Mystics and Activists* is a breath of fresh air. I found myself savoring each word and felt so connected to a greater sense of who we are as humans on this planet. It spoke deeply to my spirit and soul.

Jessica Stokes, Author, of *Seeking Clarity in the Labyrinth, A Daughter's Journey Through Alzheimer's*

FIERCE COMPASSION, DEEP DEVOTION

Poems for Mystics and Activists

MARIE DIMENNA

Red Thread Publishing LLC. 2023

Write to info@redthreadbooks.com if you are interested in publishing with Red Thread Publishing. Learn more about publications or foreign rights acquisitions of our catalog of books: www.redthreadbooks.com

Paperback ISBN: 9781-955683-500

Ebook ISBN: 9781-955683-494

Cover Design: Sierra Melcher

Contents

Dedication

This book is dedicated, with love and fond memories,
to my grandfather, John Polansky,
and my Uncle Mike DiMenna.
Though you have both passed from this world,
you always remain in our hearts.

Introduction

My friend Chanda and I initially had opposite reactions to the presidential election results of 2016. During the chilly November days following the election, I signed onto facebook a thousand times a day. Seeing my facebook friends' posts of outrage and grief helped me express my own feelings and let me know that I was not alone in my experience. Chanda, on the other hand, purposely distanced herself from news and social media. She needed to contain herself first; she just wasn't ready to see and hear what others around the country and the globe were saying about the election.

A couple weeks after the election, Chanda was ready to talk with me about Donald Trump becoming our new president. The two of us met at an Italian restaurant in St. Paul, near where we both lived. (I have since moved to Philadelphia, but at the time I was living in Minnesota). During our dinner, Chanda told me the truth about what life was like for her as a Black American. "For some people," Chanda said, "speaking out against racism is an event that happens during a moment in time, and then they return to living their lives. They have the luxury of forgetting about race as an issue. For Black Americans, race is always with you. It is always at the forefront of your mind and your thinking."

As the months passed, I often thought about my candid conversation with Chanda. I wondered if the presidential election of Donald Trump had unleashed in us Americans an honesty and willingness for authentic expression that had previously been veiled. The election results demonstrated to us so distinctly the need to speak out against racism, sexism, anti-Semitism, and all other prejudice. Perhaps my conversation with Chanda was one small piece of this collective call to honesty and sharing of ourselves with one another.

Two and a half months after the election, Donald Trump was sworn in as President. On inauguration day, I visited my massage therapist, David, for my monthly massage. David was dressed in a stylish black workout suit with a red tee-shirt underneath. I asked if he was wearing black to mourn Trump's inauguration the way one might wear black to a funeral. He replied that yes, he was wearing black to grieve the beginning of the Trump presidency.

Later that day, I had a phone appointment with my spiritual teacher, Rev. Timothy.

"Happy Friday!" he said, excitement in his voice.

"No," I said. "Not happy Friday. Condolences on Inauguration Day."

"Yes, condolences," he replied.

The tone changed the following day, January, 21st, 2017. A sense of empowerment, hope, and inspiration filled the air. Women and men all across the globe attended the Women's March as a protest against bigotry and hate. "He's not our president," they said defiantly.

I tried to participate in my local Women's March in St Paul, but fell and injured my wrist shortly after I arrived. My first thought after my fall was, *I'll march and then go to the ER.* Since I had not yet met up with the friends I planned to march with, strangers came to my aid. Three women, Camille, Jane, and Jeni, huddled around me and called 911. They were gracious with me, trying not to throw it in my face that marching would now be quite unlikely for me. I gradually surrendered to the reality that I wouldn't be marching anytime soon.

Thirty minutes after 911 had been called, a police officer arrived in a golf cart. The crowd of a hundred thousand people was far too large for the officer to bring an ambulance. The large crowd also prevented him from reaching me quickly. The officer apologized for the delay as soon as he arrived at my location. "Thank God you didn't have a life-threatening injury. I never would have made it in time," he said. He then drove me in the golf cart to the ambulance several blocks away.

Due to my injury, I never did meet up with my friends, Ashley and Chelsea. Instead, Camille, one of the women who had gathered around me after my fall, stayed with me all day in the ER. This wasn't the women's march I had planned, but Camille and I were marching in Spirit with all the courageous men and women who marched and protested that day. Truly, Camille was my good Samaritan.

She sacrificed participation in an important protest to help me.

Women helping women was what the women's march was all about, and I will always remember Camille's commitment to me after my fall. In between visits with the ER nurses and doctors, Camille and I bonded as we spoke to one another about our life stories. Camille articulated how challenging it had been when her husband passed away a few years ago. I was thankful that she could open up about her grief, even though we had just met.

When my ER doctor discharged me from the ER that evening, Camile only allowed me to ride home in an Uber without her when she decided I was well enough to make the journey home alone. She also called me throughout the next week to see how my wrist was healing. When I thanked her for her help, she simply said, "I know you'll pay it forward." I promised Camille I would indeed look for opportunities to return the favor.

I am a firm believer that protesting is far from the only activity that counts as activism. Voting, volunteering our time to help individuals, participating in neighborhood clean-ups, calling our politicians about issues that matter to us, and countless other activities can be placed under the umbrella of activism.

From the attack on the US capitol to income inequality and climate change, our nation's issues and global issues tug at our heartstrings every day. It can be easy for the problems of the world to overwhelm us. Or we can shut down emotionally and ignore the world's suffering. It's tempting to believe that nothing can be done to change social problems such as world hunger or school shootings. But our fear and resignation will not serve us or the world.

I'm not saying that we shouldn't grieve for the collective heartache. Grieving for the world's injustice is an important part of living a conscious life. But our feelings of sadness and anger at injustice and tragedy need a container. Hope in a world where each person and community are safe and cared for is the needed container for our grief.

There is a quote in the Talmud, the central text of Rabbinic Judaism, which summarizes what I wish to say in my poetry:

"Do not be daunted by the enormity of the world's grief. Do justly, now. Love mercy, now. Walk humbly, now. You are not obligated to complete the work, but neither are you free to abandon it."

In his book *The More Beautiful World Our Hearts Know is Possible*, Charles Eisenstein proposes that the world is transformed when we embrace our interconnectedness. It is our belief and our vision for the "more beautiful world our hearts know is possible" that will bring forth the new, more equitable world.

As we transition from the Age of Pisces to the Age of Aquarius, the world is experiencing a time period of great transition and change. The Aquarian Age (which will last for the next two thousand years) is marked by cooperation, collaboration, community, and individuals bringing their unique gifts and expressions to work for the greater good. All of the qualities the Aquarian Age represents are essential to birthing a new, more loving society.

Throughout my life, fostering a deep connection with God has always been coupled with serving others. Quite simply, if we love God, we will love and care for our neighbors. In addition to my poetry being a call to service and community, devotion is also at the heart of my poetry. Many of my poems can be read as prayers.

Finding time for prayer and meditation is an important part of my daily routine. Both prayer and meditation give me a sense of rejuvenation and connection with the world around me. I was raised Catholic and have identified as a Christian Mystic most of my adult life. As a mystic, I value the inner experiences and communication we have with the spiritual world. I firmly believe that no religion has a monopoly on God. Each path to God is a unique and much needed expression of God. It would be a pretty boring world if we all embraced the same theology.

So often our pain and heartbreak bring us to our knees before God. In the words of Rumi, "The wailing of broken hearts is the doorway to God." In my early twenties, my desire to be free of depression was one of the primary reasons I moved across the country from Philadelphia to Kansas City to join a close-knit mystical community. I ended up living in Kansas City for eight years until I moved to Minneapolis to continue participating in the same mystical Christian community that brought me to Kansas City. As I grew and developed over the years, my emotional pain lessened, and no longer became the driving force for my spiritual seeking. In time, simply wanting more of the love and connection I found from my relationship with God and Jesus and Mary became the primary reason for prioritizing my spiritual life.

As a mental health therapist and Christian minister, I want to walk alongside others on the healing journey. I would be of little or no help to others had I not embarked on my own path of healing. Most of the meditations and mindfulness techniques I suggest are the very same skills I used to heal from my own emotional pain.

As we heal, there is more space inside us for God's peace, love, and light. We also have more of ourselves to give. Cultivating a sense of inner peace is one of the biggest impacts we can have on the world around us.

May my poems guide you as you deepen in your relationship with yourself, others, and the divine within you.

May we each hold steadfast to believing in the more beautiful world we are co-creating together.

In the words of Rabindranath Tagore, "I slept and dreamt that life was joy. I awoke and saw that life was service. I acted, and behold, service was joy."

PART I

Compassionate Hope:
A Call to Activism

A Recovery Poem

People recover

from illness

from sorrow

from addiction

from acts of violence.

People recover

our voices joined together

in harmonic song.

People recover

from death

from persecution

from divorce

from prejudice.

People recover

with courage

and strength of character.

We hope

we dream

we dare to live again.

People recover

from abuse

from injury

from injustice

from natural disaster.

People recover

We triumph--

creating networks of support

finding one another

in the fabric of community.

People recover

from poverty

from trauma

from abandonment

from homelessness.

People recover

in time with hope

the strength to continue

lies within the core of our beings.

We recover

from mental disturbances

from loneliness

from low self-esteem

from feeling violated.

We recover

with the love and commitment

of our sisters and brothers.

We recover

from fear

from isolation

from imprisonment

from acts of terrorism.

We recover

The limitations of yesterday

shall not prevent us

from seeing and believing

in the promise of a beautiful tomorrow.

We recover

from anger

from war

from slavery

from the Holocaust.

We recover--

The desire to be well

shall make us whole again.

We recover

from hatred

from doubt

from despair

from dishonesty.

We are liberated.

We are healed.

We find mercy.

We seek love.

We find grace.

We sow seeds of compassion.

We acknowledge truth.

We witness reconciliation.

We dedicate ourselves

to loving one another.

We affirm the goodness

we see in humanity.

"A Recovery Poem" was first published in *Occupational Therapy in Mental Health* by Tana Brown. This poem is republished with permission from F.A. Davis Company.

Better in Community

Love has not been canceled

in the year 2020.

A pandemic cannot

keep us apart.

We find adventure

in our hearts and homes.

We use creativity

and innovation

to adapt and thrive.

The bread that we break

the meal that we share

family time,

our hearts' delight.

We are better together-

better in community

even when our community is virtual.

Thank God There's Real News Today

We have real news on planet Earth.

Today a family peacefully resolved conflict,
and a father made a sacrifice for his child.
Today friends laugh and cried together-
they attended a zoom funeral and wedding
all in one day.

Today mothers joined together
to speak out against injustice,
and essential workers gave their all
for their communities.
Today we celebrate

for a baby was born

and a hospice patient

found peace

before she died.

Today a couple

madly in love

celebrated their engagement

and a grocery store cashier

was given an eighty-dollar tip.

Workers united together

to gain better pay and benefits.

Activists passionately and peacefully protested

while our children made big plans to save the world.

We don't have time for fear or doubt.

Instead, we focus on the gifts of community

and pray for peace throughout the world.

Thank God there's real news today.

Thank God!

Thank God!

No Right or Wrong Path

There is no right

or wrong path

for the modern woman.

We are career women,

childfree women,

working mothers,

full-time mothers,

and retirees.

We trust each woman

has an inner knowing

guiding her to her particular path.

We can't afford *not* to change the world,

because people everywhere are suffering.

We accept our assignment humbly and boldly

as we go where no woman has gone before…

into the second millennium

hand-in-hand

as lightworkers

united in our work and mission

united in our vision

for clean drinking water,

healthcare, and schooling

for every child throughout the world.

We are fierce when we need to be-

not on our watch will

children be kept in cages.

We are gentle when the moment

calls for gentleness-

I will read you a bedtime story,

my dear.

The work of the modern woman

calls us to mother our own children

and mother ALL children.

We emulate our role models.

In 1982, Mother Teresa of Calcutta

rescued the orphans of Lebanon

during a ceasefire.

She was warned,

the risk is too great.

Of course the warning

did not stop Mother Teresa

from rescuing

the little ones abandoned,

most of them gravely ill.

No risk is too great

to save the children.

No risk is too great

to love,

protect,

and nurture the children.

We Americans

We have the same sun, stars, moon.

We have the same national parks.

We all want good things for our children.

How do we Americans begin to really

love one another?

The United States Fed the Hungry

We want to say truthfully

the United States fed the hungry

clothed the naked

and visited those in prison.

We want to say truthfully

the United States

cared for the sick

and healed their illness.

We want to say truthfully

we kept our children safe at school.

We want to say truthfully

we used our vast resources wisely.

and served well together.

The Love Which Unites Us

We pledge allegiance

to the love which unites us

rather than the fear which divides us.

Love is a binding force

binding us together.

Why wouldn't we want to serve one another?

Love is Real News

Love is real news.

Today love moves in all

of our lives.

Today people everywhere found hope,

perseverance,

and endurance

during a pandemic.

Today Americans realized they could not

be a wealthy country

if they did not adequately address

the pandemic of poverty in their land.

Real news isn't just sunshine.

It's also truth,

sobriety,

and a willingness to be honest with one another.

Light for a Shattered Democracy

Together we can change

the American healthcare system.

and American immigration.

Together we can heal

what is broken

and be light for a shattered democracy.

Enough Love in Our Hearts

There's enough love in all our hearts
to heal the world.

The world will be changed
by all the heart we give.

We are building our global village
one day,
one step at a time.

Our Worries

I worry about whether or not I packed enough food for lunch.

He worries about whether or not he'll be shot when he walks out the front door.

I worry about whether or not my shirt matches my shoes.

She worries about whether or not she has the money to feed her six children.

I worry about whether or not I have time to check my email before I head to work.

They worry about whether or not the bombings will end.

I worry about whether or not I will be stuck in traffic.

She worries about where she'll spend the night,

and whether or not the doctor will see her;

she cannot pay.

Dark Dream

A fifty-year-old woman

weeps at the bitter remembrance-

 it always remains.

The man's words crashed like thunder,

"You are not worthy to enter this pristine home."

The girl dreamed a dark dream,

"I am horrible,

not worth a dime to this man who is White."

Our Mission and Our Hope

We stand in peace.

We stand in love.

We stand in light.

We value inclusion.

We value women.

We value men.

We value non-binary people.

We value our neighbors

 all across the world

for we are our brothers' and sisters' keepers.

We value all cultures and religions.

We acknowledge with reverence

the dignity and profound beauty of humanity.

We seek to love our enemies,

as difficult as this always is.

We love all people.

Together this is our mission and our hope.

Our Nonviolent Army

The underground railroad of today

 is the love in our hearts whispering,

"I love you"

to each individual

and each group of people

who feel rejected,

who feel "less than human"

 because of intense hatred and fear.

Our nonviolent army of love

is moving forward with hope

and deep love for one another.

Global Reconciliation

We see

a world

in need of both

individual reconciliation

and global transformation

in which nations and races

greet each other

as brothers and as sisters

committed to shaping the world anew.

Union

There is a marriage

between peace and justice.

We shall have a democracy

when justice is served,

and when peace reigns throughout the land.

We cry out loudly,

please give us back our democracy.

Our democracy has been stolen from us.

We cry for our country

while rich, colorful murals

announce,

know justice

know peace.

The protestors chant,

"Show me what democracy looks like,

this is what democracy looks like."

A smile forming on their faces

as they shout in unison,

"Black lives matter,

Trans lives matter."

The protest evokes

empowerment and comradery

for all who participate.

We mourn

we heal

we work together

We know there are

miracles to behold

even in a fractured democracy.

Hope For a World to Come

Lord, help us transform the world.

From valuing money above all…to valuing us above all.

From the lack of reverence for life…to valuing each living being.

From killings with guns…to embracing a loved one in our arms.

From the destruction of our Earth…to our roles as co-creators with God.

From nuclear bombings…to global reconciliation.

From the old America…to the new frontier of inner peace.

From the clinging of fear (what we're accustomed to)…to bowing before love's altar.

From ignoring the cry…to the feeding of many.

May You Be Free

"I want to hear your anger,"

they said.

"There's grave injustice on the planet."

May you be free,

and may you be safe

from systematic racial oppression.

"We're responsible,"

they said,

"And we're truly sorry

for the trail of tears

our ancestors caused.

"Let our apology

lead to reparations,"

they cried.

"And may you be free

from systematic racial oppression.

"What do you mean

they don't believe

in systematic racial oppression?"

she cried.

May someone hold the peace.

May someone become outraged

at the war and infraction.

It's our job to hold the peace.

It's our job to transmute anger

into words of healing and grace.

You've got to be a freedom fighter

the angel of peace

and giver of mercy.

"These are tough times,"

they said.

"Thank God

you light up a school,

a theater,

and a Universe."

Thank God

more women marched than ever before.

Thank God the September 11th angels

heard our cry.

The freedom warrior

lies within your heart,

my friend,

and so does

the angel of mercy

you were destined to become.

May the silence be

the meditation,

prayer,

and vigil

during our time of need

rather than the silence

in the face of our suffering.

It's our job collectively

to end white silence.

Yesterday we filled the jails-

"We've got to be willing to fill up the jails,"

Dr. King said,

his voice reverberating throughout the land.

Today we fill the homes.

"Please stay home for us,"

they said,

a plea for safety

and concern for our fellow humans

during the pandemic.

It's the concern for our fellow human

that leads to our hope and our prayer.

May you be free,

and may all people be truly free.

19

We Seek the Promised Land

Gandhi went about the work of healing his nation's soul.

Today, we have been given a similar task,

to bring healing to the soul of our nation.

We can give money to schools,

house the homeless,

and so forth.

But if we do not work towards healing our nation's soul,

we will have the very same America.

Anyone who has done serious healing work knows

you cannot just run towards the light

hoping to catch it

or hoping it catches you.

You must first cry for all the heartaches in your life.

And so as a nation,

we must grieve and atone

for our many mistakes

such as the way throughout the centuries

we treated and are treating

Native Americans and African Americans.

In atoning,

we vow to never again make the same mistake.

We call this learning from our mistakes.

We pray that collectively we are transformed

into a loving, peaceful country

who honors and respects each soul.

May there be an initiation for our country

as we birth a new nation.

We are the forefathers and foremothers

of the new American frontier,

the land we dream of

the land we believe in whole-heartedly.

We go about the business

of recreating our country

to be the land of true freedom

and true promise.

Our American dream,

where everyone has a seat at the table

and where everyone's God-given inherent value

is acknowledged and celebrated.

We are a country

of both slave owners and abolitionists

of both peacemakers and pillagers.

Our past does not have to bind us

to hatred and despair.

Out of the ashes

we rise.

We cannot remain in bondage

to the unconsciousness of our past.

During this new millennium,

we vow to become a conscious group of people

dedicated to the inception

of the peaceful America we long for.

Evolution is propelling us forward

with hope

with vision

with compassion

with yearning.

Martin Luther King Jr.

believed in the promised land.

Moses saw the promised land,

and with our eyes

we see and we seek the promised land.

Note: This poem is based on the teachings of Marianne Williamson.

20

The Love and Blessings of Easter

There is a time period of waiting,

of hopeful anticipation

in between Good Friday and Easter.

During this time of preparation

we have already endured

the agony of the cross.

But the glory of Easter has not yet arrived.

We have mourned, persisted, and endured

the past four years.

What a glorious morning

when we welcome not only

our new president and vice-president,

but also welcome a new way

of being an American citizen

and global citizen.

In this way of being

we value one another

over profit and self-interest.

Wait for this

long for this

hope for this

new way of being

a shining light.

The new day is dawning-

we have a new president

and a bold opportunity

to create a new America.

May the labor pains of the past four years

bring forth the birth

of our collective new beginning.

There is much to celebrate today,

but reconciliation and healing are also needed.

There has been collective heartbreak,

but we thank God for the opportunity to serve together.

May the love and blessings of Easter

fill each of our hearts.

Note: This poem was written for the inauguration of

President Joe Biden.

Our Revolution

It is difficult to be patient

in the face of injustice.

Mother Teresa of Calcutta

waited two years to start her mission

of serving the poorest of the poor.

She waited for the Pope's and Archbishop's blessing.

She never tired

and consistently wrote to the Archbishop,

reminding him of her calling

to serve those in dire distress.

If you are wanting

healthcare for all people

a female president

or our second Black president-

I hear you.

The civil rights movement

and India's independence

from Great Britain

were long, arduous processes.

It took years of persistent effort

to finally see the fruits

of the activists' labor.

You don't have to support

a particular candidate

to be a part of our revolution.

You just need a really big heart.

Messages

First there was a whisper

Then, the message became louder.

Eventually, there was an earthquake.

Messages become louder when we fail to hear them.

Can we listen to the lesson of the earthquake?

Each of us receive messages and lessons

for our personal lives.

Collectively we are receiving important messages as well

that so much more can be done

for ecological healing

for climate change

for racial justice

for immigrants and asylum seekers.

Listen with wisdom

take action

vote

do your part.

No act is too small.

Every voice matters.

Every act matters.

It is imperative

that we listen and respond

to the signs of the times.

Orbit of Love and Fear

There is an orbit of fear and an orbit of love

surrounding each one of us.

We choose which orbit guides us in each moment.

Stay the course of love my friend,

even when you cannot see the path.

Breathe in the compassionate world we are co-creating.

Breathe out all that does not serve us.

Note: This poem was written following the death of George Floyd.

Real News Today

We have some REAL news today on planet Earth!

For real!

I cannot hear you when you yell,

"Fake news."

Today a daughter forgave her father.

and a five-year-old gave his allowance

to a family member in need of the funds.

Iranian school girls removed their hijabs

and bravely risked their lives

in protest against their government.

Youth all across the globe united-

urging their governments to take bold action

against climate change.

Today, friends were both

vulnerable and loving

with one another

while people everywhere

dedicated themselves to self-love.

Nothing's fake about the news today.

We got REAL news

here on planet Earth.

REAL at its very core...

real in our hearts,

in our souls,

and in our communities throughout the world.

Kind Children and Kind Adults

We encourage school kids

to befriend the lonely classmate.

Adults need to do this too.

You see the lonely neighbor

without any visitors.

Pay him a visit.

You see the parent at your

children's school

who withdraws from the other parents.

Strike up conversation.

You see the woman in your community

excluded from social events.

Invite her to the lunch you are hosting.

Offer kindness to your colleague

bullied by his supervisor.

We need kind adults and kind children.

Children are taught by our example.

We are the example of kindness and generosity

our children emulate.

Special

"You are special,"

he said.

"I see that you are struggling

with some sort of challenge or disability.

Look at me,

I have one eye,

I lost the other

in the accident at the factory.

I am special too."

Alcohol Hour

Happy hour

sad hour

happy hour

sad hour

Marie,

every night

after I turn off the TV

and hop into bed

I thank God

that not a drop of Bud

nor an ounce of wine

nor a sip of brandy

has crossed

the threshold of my mouth.

Happy hour isn't alcohol hour--

I'm not meant to live that pain.

PART II

Communion with the World and Honoring Relationships

Teacher

Elder brother

Elder sister

on this path

teach us the ways

of wisdom,

compassion,

truth,

and love.

Everything Is a Spiritual Path

I previously believed

I knew what a spiritual path entailed-

prayer, meditation,

reading spiritual texts

and ritual.

Then

I learned

I was mistaken.

It was then I realized,

everything is a spiritual path.

Dating is a spiritual path.

Our careers,

friendships,

eating meals,

physical exercise,

raising children,

and the mundane aspects of life

are all integral parts of our spiritual path.

Follow Your Path

Follow your spiritual path

wherever it leads you.

One day

my path

simply found me

and all the ways I wanted to serve

suddenly seemed possible.

With grace

the impossible is possible.

Put your heart and soul

into the work you are doing.

There are a thousand

magnificent steps

in the journey of your awakening.

One day

your path

will simply

rise up

to meet

and greet you.

Infinite Blessings

We have heard it said,

"Count your blessings."

Yet when we arrive at a place

Where we recognize

just how splendidly remarkable

life truly is

no blessings shall be counted

for it is then we shall see

that the blessings that surround us

are infinite indeed.

Gratitude Exercise

Write down in a journal

one hundred things

you are grateful for.

You will be amazed

at all the simple delights in life

you previously took for granted.

Stretch into the joy of this exercise.

What else am I grateful for?

Where does my heart find delight?

Gratitude raises our vibration

and enables us to connect

with the Universe,

the world around us,

and other human beings.

Contrast connects us to gratitude.

If we have a day in which we are sick in bed,

suddenly we are more appreciative of our health.

If we can imagine the many difficulties of being blind,

we will no longer take our eyesight for granted.

When your mind wanders,

when you find yourself in fear,

doubt,

or unconsciousness-

return to the state of amazement and thankfulness.

There's so much to be grateful for

in this rich and wondrous life.

Note: This poem is based on a sermon by Isa Tures.

Faith Is

Faith is knowing

everything will work out

for your good

and the good of others

even when you cannot see the next step

or the next leg of your journey.

Faith is trusting, hoping, and knowing

that everything will work out

for the best

even when your GPS is broken,

and you don't have a clue where you're headed.

Thank God for You

Your presence,

light

and smile

touch the lives of others.

You have amazing gifts

and are more than enough.

It is easy to doubt yourself.

Please trust me when I say,

"You make a big impact

on the world around you.

You shine brightly.

Thank God for you!"

My Hero

You always said

what was most important-

"I love you and am praying for you."

You loved us unconditionally.

Your simplicity

humility

and

poetic nature-

the gifts you gave us.

Grandpa,

you are my hero

and I will love you always.

~

Note: This poem is about my grandfather, John Polansky, who this book is dedicated to.

Your Voice

No ordinary woman

no ordinary wonder.

Your voice will be the voice of us all,

strong and triumphant.

Your voice will be the shelter of a hug,

a sweetly sung melody.

Your voice will be the warmth of your spirit,

lift high the banners and balloons.

You voice will be the voice of beloved community,

a call to live as united people.

You voice will be the song of your soul,

the depth of today is unprecedented.

Circle of Friends

We widen our circle of friends.

We include you

in this circle of friends.

We are grateful for the time we spend together.

We cherish our friendships,

sustaining us

throughout the ebbs and flows of life.

We will lift you up when times are tough,

and together we will celebrate

your joys and triumphs.

The hugs,

smiles,

laughter,

and tears

all remind us

that we love one another.

Welcome to the sisterhood-

welcome to our circle of friends.

We love you dear sister.

Friends Together

We shall cry together,

but the aching has an end.

We shall laugh together,

thank God our aching has an end.

We shall walk together

hand-in-hand

forgiving every wrong

and restoring trust in one another.

We are friends together

so together

let us trail

the marvels

of this Earth.

My Child

"My child,"

I say,

tucking you under the covers

as my mother once did for me.

"My child,

I wish I could tell you

there will never be pain in your life,

and that every story will include a fairy tale ending.

"I cannot tell you these lies

or you will believe

the illusion that life is

only full of happiness.

"Perhaps you are too young

to feel my pain

or share my grief.

But one day your tears will flow.

I will hold you in my arms that day.

Instead of saying,

'It's ok,' when it's really not,

I will say,

You are strong,

You are resilient,

and of course I love you.

"Go to sleep my little one-

your innocence a precious gift."

The Human Versus Spiritual Response To Grief

Grief and love

are bound together

in the web of life.

We grieve because we feel deeply.

We grieve because we are human.

We might not speak our question out loud

but we ask ourselves,

What does our friend need

during her moment of heartbreak?

Does my friend who lost a loved one

need a human response or spiritual response?

We might say,
"My heart goes out to you-
What you are going through is so difficult.
I am here for you anytime you need to talk."
This is the human response to grief.

Knowing that God's got us
in all seasons and circumstances
is the spiritual response to our grief.

Discern
and ask deeply inside yourself-
how do I respond?
My friend needs me,
but how and when do I show up?

Wait for what is needed to appear,
wait for the right moment
to speak your words of love to your friend.

Note: This poem is based on the teachings of grief expert David Kessler.

Healing Is Quite Possible

Trust and know

with all your heart

that your body will heal.

I want this.

There is absolute certainty

in your knowing.

Healing is not impossible.

In fact,

it is quite possible.

Trust and know

with all your heart

that your body will heal.

Healing from Heartbreak

Approach your pain

with self-compassion,

curiosity,

mindfulness,

and self-love.

Let go of self-hatred.

Begin again.

Forge a new relationship with yourself.

Kindness is the key to healing your pain.

Know you can experience freedom from this nightmare.

Embark on this courageous journey.

Cry until you have no more tears to shed.

Call on your angel and pray without ceasing.

Ask to be released from this pain.

Forgive yourself.

Forgive others.

Trust the process.

Allow wisdom to guide you

to wholeness and restoration.

You deserve to be happy.

You deserve to be free.

Your pain is crying out,

dying to be heard and witnessed.

Listen to your feelings' messages.

Heartache is only temporary.

The sun will rise again,

and you will overcome this hardship.

Your pain has a lesson to teach you.

The lessons you learn leave an imprint on your soul.

All that binds you today

will be fertile ground

for your evolution and transformation.

The Uplifting Nature of Transformation

Transformation is

the brand new lens

with which we see

the world,

ourselves,

and one another.

Transformation sings

it speaks

it stands.

Transformation is the vehicle

mobilizing our dreams

and transforming our hearts' desires

into abundant, bountiful life.

Transformation carries us

cradles us

uproots us from all darkness

breathes new life

into our beings

and enables us to soar.

The Life of Your Dreams

My present life

was the life I created

based on all my past prayers,

heartfelt desires,

and meditations.

Today I am creating my future life

with love,

true longing,

and intense hope.

If there is something you want

in your life that has not arrived,

today you are preparing and

putting things in place

for your dreams to become reality.

We do not yet see the seed

that will bud into a plant tomorrow.

It is so close to sprouting.

We just see the soil,

not the budding plant.

Trust, have faith, wait patiently.

The life of your dreams is on its way.

Each Day Is Like a Wedding Day

Treat each day

as if it's your wedding day.

Go ahead and tell a bride

she is beautiful

on an ordinary Monday.

Use your good china

on a random Tuesday.

May the joy

that lights up your heart

cause you to believe

that everyday is Christmas.

Each day is like a wedding day,

truly a special day to

remember and cherish.

Life is a miracle,

a precious gift to behold.

Life I a Bed of Roses

Whoever told you,

"Life isn't a bed of roses,"

lied to your face.

Life is a bed of roses-

the sun to nourish

the soil to provide nutrients

the stem, the connector

the thorns, to prick and pierce

the leaves, falling to the ground

each petal, a portion of the whole.

We admire and are in awe of

the rose in full bloom.

Love Knocks

Love knocks

upon the door

wherever you are

whoever you are

love awakens

the senses from slumber.

Love pries open the door

enters

never once returning

hatred born of anger.

Love

like a gentle touch

always heals

and never fails to heal.

Love is the

the eternal and sacred aspects

of life.

Love Simply Is

Beyond color

beyond creed

beyond age

Without beginning

without end

explosive healing tool

Love simply is

Worry

I never saw the sun

the stars

the moon

the clouds

the lilacs.

I never heard the birds humming

nor the silence of the winter snow.

I did not feel the gentle breeze

or sink my feet deep into the sand.

I could not read the poetry

the children did not giggle

the wind did not whistle

until I gave up worry.

The Minnesota Cold

I am learning to embrace

the Minnesota cold.

Acceptance of the winter chill

draws me to compassion

for the homeless and those who work outside.

I remind myself,

winter will change to spring

the ice will melt

the flowers will bloom.

I do not like the cold,

but I see sparkles in the snow.

I admire the beauty and stillness

of the forest transformed by the recent snowfall.

On the coldest day,

the sun is bright

On the shortest day,

the sun still shines.

On the darkest night

the Christmas lights

and stars in the nighttime sky

are our guiding lights.

The evergreen trees

a reminder

of eternal and everlasting life.

Balance

We do our best

to find balance

each day.

Balance between

work and rest

rest and play

solitude and

time spent with others.

When we feel relaxed

and rejuvenated

we have more of ourselves

to give.

There is a harmony

and synchronicity

that comes with

giving ourselves

the gifts of rest and fun.

We ask ourselves,

How do I want to use

this moment?

What would replenish me

and bring peace to my day?

Where is my joy

amidst the stress and chaos of life?

Go ahead,

give yourself

everything you need.

Learning Our Lessons

How long does it take us to learn our lessons?

It takes two times or two thousand times

We judge ourselves and others

for the time it takes to learn our lessons.

Can we patiently wait and trust

that we will

learn, grow, and develop?

Trust both the process and destination.

Let go of judgment

and be present to the unfolding journey

of your soul's knowing.

Free to Express Our True Nature

We humans are like flowers.

We open vulnerably to the world,

Not knowing if the sun

will shine on our petals

unsure if a passersby

will appreciate our particular uniqueness.

We dare to bloom,

hoping we will receive what we need.

Each experience of being

seen, acknowledged, and heard

enables us to trust it is safe

to be ourselves and let our light shine.

We are free to express our true nature
when we are received with open arms.

Values of Vulnerability and Personal Growth

Vulnerability

and personal growth and development

are underrated values in our society.

People should be applauded

for being vulnerable

and for all the ways they

have grown and transformed.

Good for you for being vulnerable.

I applaud you for the remarkable ways

you have grown and transformed.

Vulnerability is accompanied by risk,

but the risk is worth it.

The alternative is shrinking our light

and our authenticity.

Dare to be naked

with those around you.

Vulnerability exposes the real you.

We want to know and see your true self.

Let us into your heart and your life-

show us both your joy and pain.

We're willing to show you

our true selves as well.

It is our trust in one another

that leads to our intimate sharing.

Your True Nature

Who are you?

What are you identified with?

Your thoughts?

your emotions?

the expression of your true nature?

Your true nature is the pure and holy part
of your being.

Your true nature is a deeper place within you

than your thoughts and emotions.

Allow your true nature to guide you

through each day,

each obstacle,

each evolution of who you become.

Your Life Story

All the shit and beauty

occurring in your life

holds meaning,

truth,

and wisdom.

You don't have to write a memoir

to share your life story.

We can all look within

and ask,

how can my pain and my knowing

provide hope for someone else?

How can my story play a role in helping others heal?

We have heard it said,

Your deepest pain

will lead you to your service.

It is also true that

your service will

unlock your deepest joy.

The world needs your vulnerability and courage.

We need to hear your life story,

so please go ahead and share it.

Words of Wisdom About Writing

In life there are no periods.

Only commas, typos, rough drafts, and next chapters.

Dare to let someone see your rough draft

(your first rough draft).

We have heard it said,

"A picture is worth a thousand words."

Perhaps the reverse is true-

A paragraph can be worth a thousand pictures.

Find a writing community.

Tell your story through the lens of love.

Learn all there is to learn about writing.

Write, write,

and keep on writing.

Let your creative voice

fill the space,

the void,

and the pages.

You were born to write your masterpiece.

Listening

I have amazing, wonderful,

insightful, deep, and

very funny things to say.

Can you tell I am humble?

When I have so many important things

I am waiting and wanting to say,

I am not listening to the friend I am conversing with.

My friend wants to be heard, acknowledged, and seen.

All the things I have to say

are not nearly as important as listening.

Can I practice listening?

Can I remain open to the truth my friend wishes to share?

Consciousness in Our Relationships

When we bring

consciousness

into our parenting,

partnering,

teaching,

and friendships

our relationships

save the world

and are the voice of peace

ringing like a church bell

and whispering

words of love.

We dance gracefully with one another

and ask forgiveness for our shortcomings.

Each and every day

we remember: we are God's children.

We remember: we belong to God.

This remembrance is our saving grace,

leading us to peace and freedom

and drawing us into deep connection with one another.

Process of Becoming

Life is a process of becoming.

We become friends.

We become parents.

We become coaches.

We become teachers.

We become students,

and we become leaders.

We give birth and we wait patiently.

We remain with the process,

the feelings,

the depth,

the song,

and the knowing.

We stay aware and awake

so that we see the sacred beauty of life.

Moments and Seasons of Relationships

There will never be

another first date

another first kiss

or first embrace.

There will never be

another tenth year of marriage.

Be present to all the wonderful,

splendid,

messy, moments

and seasons of relationship.

Vow

Love,

show me your weakness

that I may love you not for your strength.

Love,

show me your ugliness

that I may love you not for your beauty.

Love,

I'll caress you not only in health.

Love,

grow old.

our love will flourish not only in youth.

Love, I'll be weak

love me not for my strength.

Love, I'll be ugly for you.

Love, I've been ill

many the years.

Love, I'll grow old,

you by my side.

Love, when we die,

immortal the soul.

Here is my hand;

Where is your hand?

Here is your hand.

Love Oh My Love,

You whom I trust.

Love Exchange

It is the love exchange of souls

that transports creation

towards Spirit's home

of potent love.

PART III

Dancing with the Divine: Musings of a Mystic

All The Resources Within

We have all the resources we need

within our hearts and souls.

Yet we look outside ourselves

for love

affection

and belonging.

Go within

when you are hurting.

Seek God's companionship.

God will provide

the comfort and nourishment

you long for.

Why not ask God
for the answers
to your problems?
Why not ask God
to heal you?

Of course you will look to other humans
and the external world
to fulfill you-
we all do.

Yet there will be times
other human beings will fail you
and the gold that glistens
will tarnish.

Go within to discover
the unique dance
and magic
of your divine soul.

Home Altar

Create a home altar

with the most beautiful flowers you find,

candles,

seashells,

and all the sacred objects

that remind you of God.

Your home is your refuge,

and your altar, your holy space.

Here you will worship

and call out to the divine within.

This altar,

your holy ground.

Here all your prayers and promises are received.

Allow Spirit to move and guide you

as you create this sacred space.

Your altar is your reflection

of you and your unique relationship with God.

Let your soul speak to you.

In rituals

in dreams

in poetry

in nature.

Light the candles at your altar.

Create a space,

be open,

wait silently

to hear all God wishes to impart to you.

You are accustomed to seeing yourself as unlovable.

But you are simply love on this Earth.

Drink in this love.

Rest in this love.

Be the force of love.

We are created for union with God.

Magical Stars in the Sky

Our story set

at the beginning of

the third millennium

and the arrival of the Aquarian Age.

The angels, stars, and shepherds

that so typically accompany

Christmas pageants

adore the Christ child

in the modern-day manger

Three wise men and three wise women

journeyed so far.

"It's not about how high you climb,"

they sang.

They hadn't done any climbing-

a corporate ladder or a mountain peak.

"The light is here

in this manger,"

they sang

while protestors

held picket signs

outside the church:

"You strayed too far

from Biblical text."

The heroes' journey

wasn't some verbal battle,

man versus woman.

Rather,

the wise people

came to the manger

bearing gifts of

cooperation and love for the planet emerging.

"We have no gifts to bring," they said.

"Except for the gifts

etched deep into our souls."

The pageant ends with a candlelight vigil.

The minister leading the pageant

offers hot cocoa

to the protestors outside.

"It is cold outside.

Time to go home," she says

"It's dangerous after dark."

Magical stars in the sky,

she whispers,

silently to herself.

Wise Women

Mother Mary

was the wise woman

present at the birth of Jesus.

Three wise men and wise woman,

Mother Mary.

And today,

I can't count the number of wise women

I see offering the gifts their hearts long to give.

The Light of This Season

We open our hearts

the Christmas light bursts through.

We pray the light of Christmas

fills all the broken places

in our cities,

neighborhoods,

and in our world.

Regardless of what holiday we celebrate

we welcome the birthing light

into our hearts, minds, and homes.

We bring the light of the season

to our neighbors

and even to our enemies.

There's magic and mystery

in this glorious winter season.

The light brings so much promise

to a dark, dense world.

The longest night

gives way to dawn-

a universal message for the season.

The Changing of the Seasons

The equinoxes

and solstices

the turning of the seasons-

the energy of Heaven

united with the energy of Earth.

Make room within yourself

to receive the rhythm and cycle of

the changing of the seasons.

The light of heaven

pouring down into Earth

and the energy of Earth

rising to meet Heaven.

The equinoxes

and solstices

simultaneously

the beginning

and the end

intense and powerful times

journeying with the natural world

into the next season.

The sun

the moon

the Earth

all profound roles

Attune yourself to

the changing and turning

of the seasons.

70

Mary

To be held,

held by purity.

To be healed,

healed by Mary.

To be loved,

loved by Mary.

Glory streams the tears

tears washing a tender face

cream-colored candles lit

To be held by Mary

is to be rocked,

fed, and nurtured

into the world of love.

In being loved by Mary

we return to our innocent nature.

71

Jesus, Channel of Light

Dear Jesus,

we offer you

our hearts.

we offer you

our lives.

Your light is a

channel of light and love.

You bring peace to our days

loving us as

Savior,

Friend,

Counselor,

and Father.

We pray for the wisdom and strength
to follow where you lead us.

Your love is everlasting.
It sets us free
and transforms our lives
into beautiful, bountiful
creations.

We rely daily
on your love and light.
We are your disciples,
and we vow to remain faithful to you.
We trust in your teachings,
and surrender to your love.
In the surrendering,
we find our home
in you and God.
We trust the process
of being transformed
by your light and wisdom.
Your love is our shelter

and the womb in which

we give birth

to our true nature.

My Everlasting Kingdom

The last thing I would ever want

is to place you in hell.

That violates all my laws.

My heart is sincere in forgiveness.

Come to me.

No earthly kingdom lasts.

My kingdom reigns forever.

I yearn to bring hope to those who despair.

I am light in a darkened world.

Trust, faith, and mercy are foundations.

I am the salt of the Earth.

Sit and feast at my table.

My banquet is prepared for you.

The door is always open.

You are invited as my guest.

Your heart is aching for me.

Other kingdoms perish in time.

Mine is everlasting.

Our Crucifixions and Resurrections

There are a thousand

crucifixions and resurrections

in each of our lives.

The lesson of the lotus flower

Is that the ugly, murky swamp

is fertile ground

for the most beautiful flower.

We wait patiently

for our redemption,

the symbolic three days

the cycle of death and rebirth.

We remain in Christ,

knowing there is rebirth after every death.

This is the promise you gave us

in your miraculous rising.

Mother Mary, Mary Magdalene, and John

stayed the course with you.

They were present at your

crucifixion and your resurrection.

Their profound strength

witnessing your torment.

With blood shed eyes

they cried out to you,

"It's our agony too.

We are with you on the cross,

with you even unto death."

The hope of you rising

turned into splendid joy

the day the tomb was empty.

Mary Magdalene shared the triumphant news

of your rising-

He is risen.

He is risen.

He is risen indeed.

An End to Suffering

Jesus nailed to the cross

at the front of the church

took my breath away

this past Christmas.

He had me at

I'm suffering.

I spoke to him with intensity

about how I needed

life to be difficult

as a child.

"It was the right thing

for me to suffer as a child."

It was my suffering that led me to God.

He responded.

"I don't want you to suffer any longer

Why not come down from your cross?

There's so much useless suffering on the planet.

No need to suffer any longer."

As he said this,

I saw the crown of thorns

upon his head

a tear of blood upon his face.

He had tasted vinegar upon the cross.

"Rest in the peace now," he said.

Your time of suffering is over."

Calming Your Heart

I calmed the raging sea

and I will calm the raging

in your heart.

I healed the leper and the blind man.

I will heal all your aching.

Trust in me,

follow me,

lean into my love,

have faith that my love will heal you.

One Team

Lazarus wasn't an apostle

neither were the shepherds.

Paul led after the Resurrection.

We are one team

with many teammates.

God's Calling

Each of our journeys

lead to our mission

and our service.

There is no greater joy

than to answer God's calling

to be servants here on Earth.

Oh the joy that arises in us

each time we say yes

to God's calling.

When We Work for the Lord

When we work for our Lord God Almighty

We are paid and fed in love

Rather than with mere coins.

God's Love

All I need is a drop of God's love.

God's love will sustain

ease my weariness

and quench my thirst.

Without God's love

I fall to the ground

lifeless.

Service to You

Help me be still

and know of your being

changeless and calm

changeless and calm

One in the mystery

One in the silence

One in the knowing

The quitting of the mind--

My service to You.

Know This Bliss

No need to come down to Earth yet.

Be with this elation tonight.

Who am I to feel such bliss?

Am I worthy of this divine kiss?

Your cup runeth over with all good things.

Call out to your God in gratitude-

you have overcome the weight of the world

and the fear of the ego.

Breathe, child,

the light of your being shines forth.

It is our birthright

to be intimate companions with the God who created us.

The whispers speak the truth

just as the silence speaks truth.

You were created to experience the deepest joy.

There is freedom beyond pain and suffering.

Taste this bliss.

Savor this bliss.

Give up useless striving.

Simply welcome this state-

where union with God is conceivable.

God's Altar of Love

Can I trust that I am loved by God

regardless of what happens in my life?

Can I trust that God's peace

is available to me

regardless of what is occurring in the external world?

Can I trust that the moment is exactly as it needs to be,

even when I would prefer a different moment?

Can I open to the present moment

even when heartache is present?

I will find freedom and joy

when I stop worshiping at the altar of fear

and instead worship at the altar of love.

I worship at the altar of love

when I trust I am loved by God always.

The Light of God

Close your eyes.

visualize bright, golden light

filling every cell of your body.

The light of God

will fill every pore, cell, and vein

of your body.

The light of God

will bring forth your true nature-

energize you,

invigorate you,

and bring you deep joy.

Qualities of God

Love,

light,

and life

the qualities of God.

Where there is love,

God abides.

The light we see, feel, and experience

is truly God's light.

The life within us and around us

is God's splendid creation.

Grow closer and closer to God.

Drawn near to your Creator,

and as you do

cherish your experiences

of love,

of light,

and life.

Spend each day communing with God.

God will never abandon you.

Instead, She will give you abundant life.

Called Me Beloved

I ran to the church,

the mosque

the synagogue.

I was out of breath.

I bowed before the altar

and admired the vibrant stained glass.

God spoke loudly,

"My dear child,

why did you leave my house?

I've been waiting patiently for your return,

waiting to embrace you with a hug and kiss of peace."

I replied,

"My God,

I am home now.

I promise not to leave you again,

for you are my life.

I rest in your love

and trust in your goodness.

I feel your presence,

and rely on your light."

God smiled

and called me beloved.

Reflections of God

If we are intelligent,

We are reflections of God's intelligence.

If we are beautiful,

God is the creator of all things good and beautiful.

If we are creative,

Spirit moves in us

to create art, music, and poetry.

If we are kind and generous,

we are answering God's call

to a life in service.

When we speak truth,

God inspires us to be truth tellers.

When we are honest,

we lead with vulnerability and bravery.

We are lightworkers,

we allow our divine spark to shine brightly.

Closing Prayer

Dear God,

Be with each of us as we draw closer and closer to you.

May we each grow in our love and devotion to you. Release anything within us that does not serve you and does not serve our highest good.

May we go forth into this world discerning how we can best use our skills and gifts for the betterment of the world and our local communities.

Draw to us all the people and experiences who would bring us into a deeper knowing of ourselves and you, our Creator.

May all of our relationships bless the world and provide us with learning, growth, and deep companionship.

May we each do all that we are called to do to bring healing and peace to this planet.

May we each be a shining light of hope, calling others home to your love.

May the Earth itself be healed and restored to its natural state.

May people everywhere be free to live lives of abundance, health, and peace.

May we collectively hear the cry for global transformation.

May we work for peace together one day and one step at a time.

Thank you, dear God, for loving us unconditionally. Amen.

Recommended Resources

Recommended Reading

Healing The Soul of America by Marianne Williamson

Return to Love by Marianne Williamson

The More Beautiful World Our Hearts Know is Possible by Charles Eisenstein

The Book of Joy by His Holiness the Dalai Lama and Desmond Tutu

The Christ Blueprint by Padma Aon Prakasha

Wild Mercy Living the Fierce and Tender Wisdom of the Women Mystics by Mirabai Starr

The Sophia Code by Kaia Ra

The Way of Mastery by Jeshua ben Joseph

This Much I Know is True by Mary Francis Drake

Living Buddha, Living Christ by Thich Nhat Hanh

Everything Belongs by Richard Rohr

Finding Meaning: The Six Stage of Grief by David Kessler

What Happened to You? Conversations on Trauma, Resilience, and Healing by Oprah Winfrey and Bruce Perry

When Things Fall Apart by Pema Chodron

The Gifts of Imperfection by Brene Brown

Atlas of the Heart by Brene Brown

The Way of Integrity: Finding The Path To Your True Self by Martha Beck

Unbound My Story of Liberation and the Birth of the Me Too Movement by Tarana Burke

Finding Me: A Memoir by Viola Davis

Climate a New Story by Charles Eisenstein

I Am Malala The Girl Who Stood Up For Education and Was Shot by the Taliban by Christina Lamb and Malala Yousafzai

Live Your Legacy Now by Barbara Greenspan Shaiman

Stamped From the Beginning the Definitive History of Racist Ideas in America by Ibram X Kendi

The Diary of a Young Girl by Anne Frank

Born a Crime by Trevor Noah

Long Walk to Freedom by Nelson Mandela

Come Be My Light: the Private Writings of the Saint of Calcutta by Mother Teresa

Even If Your Heart Would Listen: Losing My Daughter to Heroin by Elise Schiller

Caravan of No Despair: A Memoir of Loss and Transformation by Mirabai Starr

Tears to Triumph: The Spiritual Journey From Suffering to Enlightenment by Marianne Williamson

Recommended Films

I Am (documentary)

Burden

The Shack

Dead Man Walking

Swimmers

Forgiving Dr. Mengele

Life is Beautiful

Recommended Songs

"March" the Chicks

"People Have the Power" Patti Smith

"Good To Be Alive Today" Michael Franti

"I Am Light" India Arie

"Heal Me" Nirinjan Kaur

"A Thousand Suns" GuruGanesha Band

"Eye on the Prize" Sara Groves

"Even the Winter" Audrey Assad

"Help My Unbelief" Audrey Assad

"Change" Tracy Chapman

"Talkin About a Revolution" Tracy Chapman

"Divine Romance" Phil Wickham

"By Thy Grace" Snatam Kaur

"By Thy Grace" Krishna Das

Thank You

Thank you for embarking on this reading journey. I am grateful to be with you through these poems. If you feel moved to do so, please leave a review of this book on Amazon (amzn.to/3YcAbyp), GoodReads, or on other websites. Your reviews are greatly appreciated.

Please contact me at marie@sophiawisdom.org if you would like to hear more about my ongoing free online meditation classes and one-on-one online spiritual counseling. Please also contact me with any comments or questions about my poems.

www.mariedimenna.com

www.facebook.com/marie.dimenna

Acknowledgments

I would like to thank all those who supported and guided me in the writing and publication of *Fierce Compassion, Deep Devotion Poems for Mystics and Activists.*

The leaders of Red Thread Publishing, Sierra Melcher, Adrienne MacIain Ph.D., and Mimi Rich, guided me along each leg of the publishing and writing journey. Through Red Thread, I have learned an awful lot about the publishing process, and have also gained a community of women eager to support me and other writers. I am grateful for each member of the Red Thread community.

As published authors, Ma Devi Drake, Elise Schiller, Sidney Goldstein, and Barbara Shaiman have given me much needed advice, and I very much appreciate their guidance.

Anne Bloos and Mark Wiebe edited the first version of the introduction, and I am very grateful for the time and effort they put towards editing my writing.

I would like to thank my fellow writers Jessica Goldmuntz Stokes, Chris Chandler, Laura Zukosky and Judy Granlee-Gates for walking alongside me in the writing process, and making time to talk about the ins and outs of writing a book.

My Aunt, Joy DiMenna, has eagerly shared her expertise as an artist for the book cover design, and her talent and advice is very much valued and appreciated.

Special thanks to Caitlin Adair, Danyel Brisk, Catherine Wan, Jennifer French, Carol Rathe, Timothy Lin, Julia Mullaney, Kelsey Jopp, Cara Cairo, Alex Warner, and Ronda Reitz for reviewing my manuscript and providing encouragement and feedback.

My parents, Kathi and Rick DiMenna, and my brother, Adam DiMenna have been consistent supporters, not only during this writing adventure, but in life in general.

I am thankful for my friends, especially Angela Lightle, Raequel Madara, Rachel Sweet-Welsh, and Amanda Devercelli who have been loyal friends throughout the years.

I am also grateful for the love and support of my spiritual community, Sacred Balance. My Sacred Balance community has been my inspiration for writing about spirituality and community. Eva Hendrick has been an instrumental part of the weekly meditations I host each week, and I so grateful for the opportunity to get to know her. I am truly grateful for my spiritual teachers Ma Devi Drake and Beatrice Borden, who have pointed me towards a deeper relationship with God and have stood by me in the process of becoming a minister.

I would also like to thank Sandi Cohen for being a spiritual mentor and encouraging me to continue writing poetry when I was in high school.

About the Author

Marie DiMenna is a creative writer, therapist, social worker, and ordained minister in the Christian Mystical tradition. Her poem, a "Recovery Poem" is published in *Occupational Therapy in Mental Health* by Tana Brown. *Fierce Compassion, Deep Devotion* is Marie's first book. Marie currently resides in Philadelphia.

www.mariedimenna.com

facebook.com/marie.dimenna

About the Publisher

Red Thread Publishing is an all-female publishing company on a mission to support 10,000 women to become successful published authors and thought leaders. Through the transformative work of writing & telling our stories we are not only changed as individuals, but we are also changing the global narrative & thus the world.

www.redthreadbooks.com

facebook.com/redthreadpublishing

instagram.com/redthreadbooks

Made in the USA
Middletown, DE
10 April 2023